PEOPLE IN THE NEWS

Jennifer Hudson

Singer, Actress, and Voice for Change

By Edna McPhee

Portions of this book originally appeared in
Jennifer Hudson by Cherese Cartlidge.

LUCENT
PRESS

Published in 2020 by
Lucent Press, an Imprint of Greenhaven Publishing, LLC
353 3rd Avenue
Suite 255
New York, NY 10010

Designer: Deanna Paternostro
Editor: Molly Seeley

Library of Congress Cataloging-in-Publication Data

Names: McPhee, Edna, author.
Title: Jennifer Hudson : singer, actress, and voice for change / Edna McPhee.
Description: New York : Lucent Press, [2020] | Series: People in the news |
  Includes bibliographical references and index.
Identifiers: LCCN 2019018239 (print) | LCCN 2019020081 (ebook) | ISBN
  9781534568334 (ebook) | ISBN 9781534568327 (library bound book) | ISBN
  9781534568310 (pbk. book)
Subjects: LCSH: Hudson, Jennifer, 1981– —Juvenile literature. |
  Singers—United States—Biography—Juvenile literature. | Motion picture
  actors and actresses—United States—Biography—Juvenile literature.
Classification: LCC ML3930.H82 (ebook) | LCC ML3930.H82 M4 2020 (print) |
  DDC 782.42164092 [B]—dc23
LC record available at https://lccn.loc.gov/2019018239

Printed in China

Some of the images in this book illustrate individuals who are models. The
depictions do not imply actual situations or events.

CPSIA compliance information: Batch #BW20KL: For further information contact Greenhaven Publishing LLC, New York,
New York at 1-844-317-7404.

Please visit our website, www.greenhavenpublishing.com. For a free color
catalog of all our high-quality books, call toll free 1-844-317-7404 or fax
1-844-317-7405.

Foreword

We live in a world where the latest news is always available and where it seems we have unlimited access to the lives of the people in the news. Entire television networks are devoted to news about politics, sports, and entertainment. Social media has allowed people to have an unprecedented level of interaction with celebrities. We have more information at our fingertips than ever before. However, how much do we really know about the people we see on television news programs, social media feeds, and magazine covers?

Despite the constant stream of news, the full stories behind the lives of some of the world's most newsworthy men and women are often unknown. Who was Lady Gaga before she became a star? What does LeBron James do when he is not playing basketball? What inspires Lin-Manuel Miranda?

This series aims to answer questions like these about some of the biggest names in pop culture, sports, politics, and technology. While the subjects of this series come from all walks of life and areas of expertise, they share a common magnetism that has made them all captivating figures in the public eye. They have shaped the world in some unique way, and—in many cases—they are poised to continue to shape the world for many years to come.

These biographies are not just a collection of basic facts. They tell compelling stories that show how each figure grew to become a powerful public personality. Each book aims to paint a complete, realistic picture of its subject—from the challenges they overcame to the controversies they caused. In doing so, each book reinforces the idea that even the most famous faces on the news are real people who are much more complex than we are often shown in brief video clips or sound bites. Readers are also reminded that there is even more to a person than what they present to the world through social media posts, press releases, and interviews. The whole story of a person's life can only be discovered by digging beneath the surface of their public persona, and that is what this series allows readers to do.

The books in this series are filled with enlightening quotes from speeches and interviews given by the subjects, as well as quotes and anecdotes from those who know their story best: family, friends, coaches, and colleagues. All quotes are noted to provide guidance for further research. Detailed lists of additional resources are also included, as are timelines, indexes, and unique photographs. These text features come together to enhance the reading experience and encourage readers to dive deeper into the stories of these influential men and women.

Fame can be fleeting, but the subjects featured in this series have real staying power. They have fundamentally impacted their respective fields and have achieved great success through hard work and true talent. They are men and women defined by their accomplishments, and they are often seen as role models for the next generation. They have left their mark on the world in a major way, and their stories are meant to inspire readers to leave their mark, too.

Sweet Home Chicago

The city of Chicago, Illinois, began as a settlement in the early 1790s and would eventually become the third-largest city in the United States. Named for the Algonquin word *shikaakwa*, which means "wild onion" or "wild garlic"—which grew along the shores of Lake Michigan—the place that would become Chicago was originally populated by a Native American tribe called the Potawatomi. Chicago's founder, Jean Baptiste Point du Sable, a French African man, had a friendly and warm relationship with the tribe and married a local woman, Kitiwaha. However, in 1833 (the year of the city's official founding), the local tribes were forcibly removed from their land, and settlers took it over completely.

It was not all smooth sailing for the city, despite its rapid growth and position as a key transportation and shipping hub. In 1871, the Great Chicago Fire destroyed an enormous section of the downtown area, killing 300 people and leaving 100,000 homeless. Despite the tragedy, this event allowed the city to usher in a new era of architectural creativity and growth; it was in Chicago that the steel-framed high-rise was invented, allowing for the development of the kinds of skyscrapers we see in modern cities. Today, the city is known for its music, food, sports, and beautiful architecture.

Like the city that raised her, Jennifer Hudson has tasted her share of triumph and borne her share of tragedy. From her 2004 appearance on the television show *American Idol*, where she made it to the semifinals before being voted off the show, to the unimaginable personal loss of three family members to fatal domestic violence, to Hudson's growing work as an artist-activist, she has lived a life full of both the sweet and the sour. Growing up on

Jennifer Hudson was born in Chicago, Illinois, in 1981 and continued to live there long after her career took off.

the South Side left a mark on Hudson that helped to shape her: "Home is Chicago,"[1] she told talk show host David Letterman after the release of her first film, *Dreamgirls,* in 2006. Indeed, the first house she purchased, bought the same year *Dreamgirls* hit theaters, is in Chicago: "Chicago has shaped me in many ways, which is why I still live here to this day. People are always like, 'You live in L.A.? You live in New York?' I'm like, 'No. I live in Chicago.'"[2]

Hometown Hero

Jennifer Hudson grew up in a white, two-story house on the 7000 block of South Yale Avenue in Chicago. Despite the opportunity that Hudson's success brought to her family, they continued to live in this same house even after she became famous. Her family, especially her mother, did not want to leave their beloved home, their familiar neighborhood, their friends, or their church. The draw of this environment was so strong that even with the demands placed on her time—with her busy schedule of filming, recording, touring, and promoting her many projects—Hudson returned often to visit her family home. She continued to visit her family frequently in Chicago after she became a celebrity, and as her cousin Krista Nichols-Alston noted, "When she comes in, she's just Jenny Gal. She's just Jennifer."[3]

The love between Hudson and her hometown is well-documented. Chicago declared March 6, 2007, to be Jennifer Hudson Day. Her old high school, Dunbar Vocational Career Academy, has also honored her by creating a Jennifer Hudson Room, which is filled with *Dreamgirls* posters and mementos of Hudson's stint on *American Idol.* Hudson returned these favors during a December 2009 holiday special on ABC called *Jennifer Hudson: I'll Be Home for Christmas.* In the special, she refers to Chicago as the best place to be. "It is the greatest city in the world at Christmas,"[4] she declared.

It is no wonder that Hudson identifies so strongly with this remarkable place, for she is a remarkable woman. History has seen Chicago pass through extreme highs and extreme lows; it would see Hudson pass through the same. However, time and time again, Hudson has shown the same stubborn resiliency of the city that raised her. Her courage, resolve, and deep faith have helped her to remain strong when she has been faced with professional disappointment and personal tragedy.

Back to
the Start

If Jennifer Hudson's parents had known she was destined to be a singer, it would have seemed that life gave her something of a poor start. Born with underdeveloped lungs, Jennifer was small for her age, shy, and sensitive, crying often and easily. However, this rocky start was the foundation on which she would build a career. As she grew bigger, both her personality and her lungs got stronger. It quickly became apparent that she was drawn irresistibly to the music of the world around her, both in church and in everyday life.

This love of music would be one of Jennifer's greatest joys as she spent her childhood in Chicago. The Hudson home was filled with music; her parents and siblings all loved to sing, and this love fostered Jennifer's own hopes for a career in music. Both at home and at church services, music was a constant presence. The Hudsons were a big, tight-knit group—her grandmother, Julia; her mother, Darnell; her father, Samuel; her brother, Jason; her sister, Julia; and a host of extended family who lived nearby. In the comfort, joy, and safety of this bond, Jennifer was able to flourish both musically and personally.

The Comforts of Home

Jennifer Kate Hudson was born on September 12, 1981. She was the youngest child of Darnell Donerson, who worked as a secretary. Jennifer's father, Samuel Simpson, was a bus driver in Chicago.

The house that Jennifer grew up in was home to herself, her parents, and her two older siblings, Julia and Jason. They lived in a neighborhood called Englewood, on the South Side of Chicago, which suffered from high rates of both crime and poverty after decades of economic disinvestment—a stretch of time in which jobs became scarce and the population fell, creating a depressed environment. Englewood became what is called a "food desert" or "food swamp," which is a place in a city that lacks access to grocery stores and may have only cheap, unhealthy food from convenience stores. Despite the neighborhood's struggles, the Hudson family found home and community in Englewood, and Jennifer's childhood there was largely a happy one.

The family lived very modestly. Like the other families in their neighborhood, they did not have a lot of money. In spite of this, Darnell and Samuel were able to provide for their children and live relatively comfortably. Their house, while older and a little plain, was very roomy, with two stories and nine bedrooms. Later, Hudson looked back on her childhood and recalled, "We were poor but we thought we were rich, because we had everything we needed."[5]

Jennifer, her siblings, and her parents had a warm and loving home life. Both parents took active roles in the children's daily lives, providing the guidance and direction needed to keep their children safe and happy. Hudson later described her mother's loving care: "I remember when my mom used to sit and bounce me on her knee. I used to itch a lot, and to put me to sleep she would have to scratch me. She had so much patience."[6]

The thing Hudson recalls most about her family life is the music. The radio or stereo was always on, and her family members loved to sing, especially her mother and grandmother. The family was also very religious, praying together and discussing their faith at home. They took trips around the country, as a family and with their church, and Jennifer was able to see a bit of the world beyond her life in Chicago. She was growing up in the warm, protective bubble of her family and her faith, but these trips were proof that there was a wider world waiting for Jennifer Hudson to make her mark.

Music in Her Blood

Faith and religion were an important part of life for Jennifer's family, and this was expressed most obviously in their regular appearances at Sunday church services. They attended Chicago's Pleasant Gift Missionary Baptist Church every week, sometimes twice a week. One of Jennifer Hudson's favorite things about this part of her life was the music, especially the singing.

Even as an infant, Jennifer's love of music was evident. One of the stories her mother most enjoyed telling others was the time when eight-month-old Jennifer was in church during a choir practice. The choir was trying to hit a high note but could not quite reach it. Baby Jennifer, however, chimed in and hit the note perfectly. At that point, her godmother, Debra Nichols Windham, said to Darnell, "Mark my words, this child is going to sing."[7]

An important early influence on Jennifer's singing, as well as on her deep faith, was her maternal grandmother, Julia Kate Hudson. Some of Jennifer's earliest memories are of singing on her grandmother's knee at home. Her grandmother had a strong singing voice with a wide range, and Jennifer seemed to have inherited her talent and rich voice. Her grandmother, who sang in the soprano section of the church choir, also instilled in her a passion for singing that helped her overcome her shyness by encouraging her to sing at home and in church. Her growing confidence in her voice and ability allowed her to feel more comfortable outside of music as well.

Jennifer's grandmother was her musical role model, her greatest supporter, and even her first music teacher. The two of them would sit together and take turns singing songs from the choir to each other. Before long, seven-year-old Jennifer joined the soprano section and was singing alongside her grandmother in church. Together, they attended choir practice every Sunday and Tuesday, fostering a work ethic that would serve Jennifer well later in her career.

Hudson was extremely close to her family growing up, and it was their support that allowed her to focus on her dream of becoming a singer.

Finding Meaning in Music

Though only seven years old when she joined the church choir, Jennifer already knew she wanted to be a singer when she grew up. She begged the choir director, the pastor, and the organist to let her sing solos, but they felt she was too young for such a responsibility. She later recalled sitting in the bathroom of her house as a young girl and crying because she was not given the solo opportunity she so longed for, believing it was because no one wanted to hear her voice. To make up for the lack of spotlight in the choir, Jennifer entertained herself and fulfilled her dreams of stardom by singing to herself in the bathroom. Jennifer's determination to be a star was apparent to all around her. Her sister, Julia, recalled years later, "All Jennifer wanted to do was sing—and be famous."[8]

Jennifer's persistence and determination paid off when she was eventually given the choir solos she had craved. Her first solo was the hymn "Must Jesus Bear the Cross Alone." Though it was the very thing she had worked and longed for, the song did not go as smoothly as she had hoped: Halfway through, she stumbled and forgot the words. She managed to cover her embarrassment, and the mishap did not stop her from continuing to sing hymns at church. Perhaps the incident served to remind her that nothing worth having comes easy; rather than giving up on her dream, she continued to sing and audition for the solos, displaying at a young age the strong will and confidence that would play a big part in shaping her life as an adult.

Like the rest of her family, Jennifer was an avid churchgoer with a strong faith. The regular church services and choir practices helped to instill in her the values of hard work and clean living. Although her family lived in a rough neighborhood, where it would have been easy—and, for some, a necessary survival tactic—Jennifer managed to stay clear of trouble. Growing up, she did not drink, smoke, or do drugs. "I never have and I never plan on it,"[9] she later told an interviewer. Later in life, reflecting on how one's circumstances growing up can affect their opportunities as an adult, she realized that the support and love of her family gave her the tools and the chance to make dif-

Singing in the church choir was a vital part of Hudson's formation as a singer, performer, and person of faith.

R-E-S-P-E-C-T

One of Jennifer Hudson's favorite recording artists is Aretha Franklin, known as the Queen of Soul. The daughter of a Baptist minister, Franklin grew up singing in church, where she developed her gospel style and powerful singing voice—much like Hudson would, 30 years later.

Franklin's first big hit was a blues ballad titled "I Never Loved a Man (the Way I Love You)," released in 1967. The song reached number nine on the pop charts and number one on the rhythm and blues charts. Her biggest hit, which became her signature song, is the rhythm and blues classic "Respect," which was also released in 1967. The song became associated with both the civil rights movement and the women's movement. In fact, Franklin's career is known as much for her extraordinary musical talent as it is for her contribution to the political movements of her time; she believed in equality and never stopped being a force for its advancement.

ferent choices than many others in neighborhoods like hers. She said, "My family supported me, especially my mother. She would always say, 'Whatever makes you happy is what I want you to do.'"[10]

Hudson credits her involvement with the choir with something else as well. Learning to sing in the church helped her to develop her belting, gospel style of singing. She says that church will always be her favorite place to sing, and she points out that many great singers got their start singing in church, just as she did. To her—and to many others, as well—singing in church provides a sense of meaning. Hudson said, "The church [is] where I found my voice."[11]

Aretha Franklin was called the Queen of Soul because of her powerful voice, moving lyrics, and commanding stage presence.

In 1987, Franklin became the first female artist to be inducted into the Rock and Roll Hall of Fame. She also sang "God Bless America" at Barack Obama's presidential inauguration in 2009. Franklin passed away on August 16, 2018, at the age of 76.

Music for the Soul

Jennifer always knew that her future would be filled with creativity of one kind or another. Darnell inspired and encouraged all her children's creativity through hobbies and extracurricular activities in the arts. Jennifer's brother, Jason, took piano lessons, and Jennifer studied ballet. She also had a chance to model, appearing in the catalog for the Chicago Sears store at age five. In addition, Jennifer explored her creative side through drawing and writing songs.

It was music, however, that interested Jennifer the most. In later years, she would give credit to her grandmother for inspiring her singing career. In part, this was due to the many hours they would spend singing together, at home and at church, but also critical in Jennifer's musical development was absorbing her grandmother's musical tastes. Hudson has always liked listening to the artists that her grandmother and mother grew up listening to; her favorite styles of music include rhythm and blues, gospel, and pop. As a child, she sang along with soul greats Aretha Franklin, Gladys Knight, and Patti LaBelle. She also liked listening to the music of gospel singers like Mahalia Jackson, Shirley Caesar, Tramaine Hawkins, and Lucretia Campbell.

As Jennifer got older, her musical tastes expanded to artists like Whitney Houston, Celine Dion, and Destiny's Child. The first CD she ever bought was *Just the Beginning*, which was released in 1992 by the rhythm and blues group Voices and included the single "M.M.D.R.N.F. (My Mama Didn't Raise No Fool)." Her favorite songs to sing as a child and a teenager included "Inseparable" (Natalie Cole), "Neither One of Us" (Gladys Knight), and "I Believe in You and Me" (Whitney Houston).

One of Jennifer's favorite television programs was *Soul Train*. The program was a showcase of popular and enduring artists, and it was often thought of as a celebration of black excellence. Conceived by radio announcer Don Cornelius, the show was designed to look and feel like a dance club, showing off a side of America that was not often remarked on or noticed by mainstream television programming.

A Star in the Making

Jennifer's first public singing performance outside of church occurred when she was still a child and sang at her great-great-grandmother's 91st birthday party. Her family and friends who attended the party were impressed by the little girl's voice and told her it was a gift; Jennifer would come to consider that gift to be from God.

As Jennifer moved into high school, she discovered further opportunities to sing by attending the Dunbar Vocational Career Academy, a public school that focuses on preparing students to pursue various careers, including those in the arts. The acad-

All Aboard the Soul Train

Like Jennifer Hudson, the American musical variety show *Soul Train* got its start in Chicago. The show, which was hosted by Don Cornelius, aired from 1971 to 2006 and featured music as well as dancing. The show was notable for providing viewers a window into black culture—young people, both black and white, tuned in for the latest styles in music, dance, and fashion.

During its 35 years on the air, *Soul Train* featured guest appearances by hundreds of well-known singers and celebrities. The show's guest list included Paula Abdul, Christina Aguilera, the Black Eyed Peas, Mary J. Blige, Mariah Carey, Sean Combs, Destiny's Child, Jamie Foxx, Aretha Franklin, Whitney Houston, Michael Jackson, Gladys Knight and the Pips, Patti LaBelle, Ludacris, OutKast, Queen Latifah, Usher, and hundreds of others. Each episode of *Soul Train* ended with the catch phrase "We wish you love, peace and soul!"[1]

1. Quoted in Steve Jones, "It's the 'Sooouuuulll Train' Documentary! On VH1, Honey!," *USA Today*, February 7, 2010. www.usatoday.com/life/music/news/2010-02-05-soultrain05_ST_N.htm.

emy counts among its alumni such well-known performers as Lawrence Tureaud (better known as Mr. T), Lou Rawls, and Cleotha and Pervis Staples of the Staple Singers. For Jennifer Hudson, too, the Dunbar Academy would lead to bigger and better things.

Although Jennifer did not date much in high school, her warm, friendly personality and good sense of humor made her well-liked by the other students. She was a favorite among her teachers and did well academically, earning good grades and honor roll distinctions her sophomore, junior, and senior years.

Growing up, Hudson had many people who nurtured and believed in her, and their support would help her fulfill her dreams.

At this time, a family member once again exerted great influence over Jennifer's singing career. This go around it was her cousin Shari Nichols-Sweat, who was one of the music teachers at Dunbar. Hudson later said of her, "She was definitely one of my role models ... She believed in me so much—it was like an amazing support system."[12] Nichols-Sweat was very impressed by the charismatic quality of Jennifer's voice and worked with her to develop it further. With the encouragement of her cousin, Jennifer joined the school's spirit choir. It was a decision that would change the course of her life.

Jennifer quickly became the star of her high school choir and began expanding her world by performing in school musical productions. Her performances helped to make her very popular, and her classmates voted her the most talented female musician in school. Her choral teacher, Richard Nunley, was also impressed by her voice. He taught her classical singing techniques because he wanted her to develop her voice so she could sing any style of music she desired. Jennifer used that work ethic instilled in her by her grandmother and worked hard to master classical singing. Nunley said later, "She's also a great classical singer, and a lot of people don't know that."[13]

It was while she was a student at Dunbar that Jennifer made a promise to both herself and her choral teacher. As Nunley recalled later, she told him on several different occasions, "I'm going to make you proud of me. I'm going to be a famous singer."[14]

Singing in the school's choir was only the beginning for Jennifer Hudson. She seized every opportunity to develop her talent and build the foundation for an exciting career. The love, support, and guidance of her extended family and her teachers while she was growing up helped Jennifer to overcome her childhood shyness and believe in her voice—and herself.

Chapter Two

Chasing
a Dream

If there was anything that Jennifer Hudson's childhood taught her, it was the power of hard work and having faith in yourself and in the ones you love. She had made a promise to her high school choral teacher that she would use her voice to make him proud, and she intended to keep it. As the years went on, she grew more and more confident in her talent and her future as a professional musician. School performances were just the beginning; Jennifer would soon have an experience that would open her worldview even wider.

Work and Play

When Jennifer was 16 years old, she got a job at the Burger King restaurant at Eighty-Seventh and State Streets in Chicago. Her sister, Julia, worked there and had helped Jennifer get hired. Julia really liked her job there, so Jennifer expected she would too. She soon found, however, that the fast-food environment was not to her liking. She hated the long, tedious hours she spent in the restaurant. In addition, she felt like she was wasting what she had long thought of as her gift: her singing talent. Before long, Jennifer gave her notice to the restaurant manager and quit her job at Burger King.

Although her job in the fast-food industry was short-lived, it was still a good experience for Jennifer, teaching her that singing was not just her pie-in-the-sky dream job, but in fact, was a tangible goal worth working toward. She would not be happy working in another field; she had the drive, talent, and work ethic to do something she loved for a living.

Not content to wait until her high school graduation, she began to perform outside of school and church. A childhood friend, Walter Williams, helped promote her around town, and together, they created a trajectory that would help train Jennifer for a career in music and theater. She entered talent shows and performed in community musical productions. She sang at any and every event she could, just to get the experience and the exposure. She also performed in gay bars and drag clubs (places where people use clothes and makeup to challenge and explore ideas of gender, especially womanhood), although she was underage. At the same time, she continued to sing regularly in the choir, both at church and at school. Despite the time and attention these activities took, Jennifer kept up her grades and graduated from Dunbar Vocational Career Academy with honors in 1999. Though still young, she had already gained a great deal of experience singing in public and was a regular on the local music scene.

Times They Are A-Changing

Around this same time, several significant events occurred in Jennifer's personal life. First, she and the rest of her family were greatly saddened by the death of her beloved maternal grandmother, Julia Kate Hudson, in 1998. Julia had not only been Jennifer's mentor and first music teacher, she had also helped coach Jennifer for the talent shows and for her roles in community musical productions while she was in high school.

Jennifer Hudson is a graduate of Dunbar Vocational Career Academy, named in honor of African American poet, novelist, and playwright Paul Laurence Dunbar.

Today, Jennifer says she still thinks of her grandmother when she sings. She views her powerful singing voice as a gift from her late grandmother, and she sees her career as a tribute to her. One of her grandmother's favorite songs to sing was "How Great Thou Art." Jennifer keeps a recording of African American gospel singer Mahalia Jackson singing this well-known hymn, and she thinks of her grandmother whenever she listens to the song. In addition, she says that she often thinks of her grandmother right before a performance in order to build up her emotions and to inspire herself. She says she knows how proud her grandmother would be of her and is motivated by the thought, "What if she could see me now?"[15]

The year after losing her grandmother, Jennifer and her family suffered another loss when Samuel Simpson died of cancer. Along with Darnell, Samuel had provided a loving and supportive family environment for his kids, and his loss was deeply felt by all those who loved him.

On a brighter note, Jennifer began a long-term relationship with James Payton in 1999. James, a maintenance engineer, was her brother's best friend, and she had known him since she was 13 years old. They began dating around the time she graduated from high school, and the couple remained together throughout Jennifer's early career.

Another bright moment in Jennifer's personal life came in 2001. That year, her sister, Julia, gave birth to a baby boy. Jennifer doted on her new nephew, who was named Julian in honor of his mother and great-grandmother.

Moving On Up

Soon after Jennifer and James Payton began dating, their relationship faced a challenge: They were separated from each other by several hundred miles. After graduating from high school, Jennifer left Chicago for Langston, Oklahoma. There, she attended Langston University, a historically black college that has one of the top choral programs in the nation. Always a good student, she enjoyed attending her classes. However, she was not entirely happy at Langston. It was her first time so far away from home,

Jennifer began dating James Payton, her brother Jason's friend, in 1999.

and she was terribly homesick. She missed her family and her boyfriend. In addition, Langston is a rural town, which is very different from urban Chicago.

To be closer to home, she decided to transfer to Kennedy-King College, a two-year community college in Chicago. At Kennedy-King, Jennifer took some general music classes but chose not to major in music because she believed teaching was the only career a degree in music would allow, and she did not want to be a music teacher. In fact, she was more interested in the art classes that she took, in part because she had always liked drawing.

While attending Kennedy-King, Jennifer soon became an in-demand paid singer at various clubs and functions around Chicago, including weddings, birthday parties, and graduations. She also sang at her uncle's funeral parlor during services. During college, she thought that if her career as a singer did not work out, she might like to work at the funeral home as a mortician!

Taking the Leap

As it turned out, Jennifer had not needed to worry about a backup career choice; in January 2001, while still attending Kennedy-King College, she auditioned for a part in a musical that was to play at Chicago's Marriott Lincolnshire Theatre, one of the city's professional regional theaters. The musical was *Big River*, written by singer-songwriter Roger Miller. Known for his honky-tonk country music and novelty comedy songs, *Big River* was something of a creative departure for Miller, who had never written a musical before. Originally performed on Broadway and winner of a Tony Award for Best Musical in 1985, *Big River* is based on Mark Twain's 1884 novel, *Adventures of Huckleberry Finn*, which is often referred to as the "great American novel." Twain's classic is set in various places along the Mississippi River and depicts aspects of society in the American South before the American Civil War—most particularly, the relationships between blacks and whites. The setting of the novel is reflected in the bluegrass- and country-style music in *Big River*.

Jennifer was thrilled to learn she had succeeded at her audition and was cast as a singer and actor in the musical. Her belting, bluesy voice was well suited to the production's musical style. Although she had only a small singing part with no spoken lines, the role provided her with both professional stage experience and acting credentials. Jennifer later described the experience as a defining moment for her: "That's when I knew I could actually make a living doing this."[16]

That realization led to an important decision for Jennifer. Landing a role in *Big River* was the kind of opportunity she had dreamed of since she was a little girl, so she decided to leave college and instead pursue her career as a singer and an actress. She explained that she saw college as a road to a career, and when this opportunity to be in a musical presented itself, "I believed in myself and went for it."[17] Jennifer was now able to focus entirely on her career, and she stayed with the production of *Big River* for its entire run of nearly two years.

Setting Sail

Big River was a wonderful experience for Jennifer. It gave her a taste of what life as a professional singer was like and empowered her to dedicate her life to pursuing even greater heights. As the production neared its final days, she sought other theatrical opportunities in which she could showcase and further develop her singing talent. She found such an opportunity with the Disney Cruise Line.

In the fall of 2002, Jennifer auditioned for a show that was to be performed aboard the *Disney Wonder*. The show, *Hercules: The Musical*, was based on the 1997 Disney movie *Hercules*. After her audition, Jennifer was awarded her first major role, that of Calliope. Calliope is the narrator and head muse, guiding the audience through the story of Hercules. In Greek mythology, Calliope was the muse of heroic poetry and is usually associated with Homer, who is credited with writing the *Iliad* and the *Odyssey*.

From February through July 2003, Jennifer sailed on the *Disney Wonder* and performed as Calliope in the ship's musical. Performing on a ship posed certain unique challenges, as Jennifer soon discovered. Keeping her balance on a moving ship while in

A job with the Disney Cruise Line was Jennifer's first time working for Disney, but she would return to perform with and for the company many times.

Mickey at Sea

The Disney Cruise Line is owned and operated by Walt Disney Parks and Resorts, a division of the Walt Disney Company, and is headquartered in Celebration, Florida. Created in 1995, the cruise line consists of four ships: the *Disney Magic* and the *Disney Wonder*, in service during Jennifer's time as a cast member; the *Disney Dream*, christened in 2011; and the *Disney Fantasy*, which joined the line in 2012. Each of the family-friendly ships contains 900 staterooms and has special areas for different age groups, including young children, teenagers, and adults. There are many differences in the way the ships are decorated, however. The *Disney Magic*, for example, features the figure of Sorcerer Mickey at the bow (front of the boat) and a painting of Goofy at the stern (rear of the boat). The interior of the ship is decorated in art deco style, with sleek, modern lines. The *Disney Wonder*, aboard which Jennifer Hudson sailed in 2003, has a figure of Steamboat Willie at the bow and a painting of Donald Duck and his nephew Huey on the stern. The interior of the ship is decorated in an art nouveau style, with fanciful, swirling wave designs. The statues in each lobby are also different: For example, the *Disney Magic* features Helmsman Mickey, and the *Disney Wonder* features Ariel from *The Little Mermaid*.

a costume that included very high heels and a huge wig took some getting used to. The constant motion—and commotion—of living aboard a ten-deck floating city with more than 3,300 passengers and crew also took some adjusting to, even when she was not in costume. She persevered, however, and entertained aboard the *Disney Wonder* for six months. During that time, she thought of herself as part of the "Disney family," which helped her to cope with missing her own tight-knit family back in Chicago. She loved the live performances and found it thrilling to be able to sing in front of thousands of people—and to be paid to do it. In many ways, her time aboard the *Disney Wonder* prepared her for life in the fishbowl of fame—which was right around the corner, although she did not know it at the time.

If You Can See It, You Can Be It

It is vital that young people have role models who look like them and show them the pathways to what is possible. For Jennifer Hudson, who had always been a fan of popular music, one of these people was Beyoncé Knowles. During the time she sailed on the *Disney Wonder*, Hudson saw a roadmap to her own dream in the form of a solo album released by Beyoncé, who was originally part of one of Jennifer's favorite groups, Destiny's Child.

In the summer of 2003, Beyoncé released her debut solo album. Titled *Dangerously in Love*, the album produced the hits "Crazy in Love" and "Baby Boy." Jennifer loved to sing along with these hit songs, and the album soon became one of her favorites. She also took note of Beyoncé's burgeoning career as both a singer and an actress. Jennifer greatly admired and respected Beyoncé's talent and success and wanted a similar career for herself. Jennifer always clung to the idea that her potential matched with her iron will would pull her through: "Don't block your blessings. Don't let doubt stop you from getting where you want to be ... I refuse to let anyone interrupt the vision I have for myself."[18]

Jennifer was also closely following the careers of several new artists, among them Kelly Clarkson, Ruben Studdard, and Clay Aiken. Clarkson released her debut album, *Thankful*, in the spring of 2003. The album spawned several hit songs and went on to sell 4.5 million copies worldwide. Studdard released his first single, "Flying Without Wings," in the summer of 2003, and the song reached the number two spot on the Billboard Hot 100 chart. The number one spot on the chart was held by "This Is the Night," which was the debut single of Clay Aiken and

Jennifer would get the chance to work with one of her musical idols, Beyoncé, in what would become the defining project of her career.

Queen Bey

One of the artists Jennifer Hudson most wanted to emulate was singer, songwriter, actress, and fashion designer Beyoncé Knowles. Born in Houston, Texas, in 1981—the same year as Hudson—Beyoncé entered many singing and dancing competitions at a young age. She gained widespread fame with the formation of the rhythm and blues girl group Destiny's Child in the late 1990s. As the lead singer, Beyoncé helped the group become one of the top-selling girl groups in music history. In 2003, Beyoncé released the solo album *Dangerously in Love*, which won five Grammy Awards. As of 2019, Beyoncé has received 23 Grammy Awards, making her the second-most honored female artist by the Grammys.

In recent years, Beyoncé has become best known for the ways that her art and her activism intersect. Her 2016 visual album *Lemonade* explored the intersection between race, gender, and American popular culture. It also dug through her own relationship struggles with her husband, rapper JAY-Z.

In 2018, the couple released a joint album, titled *Everything Is Love*, which explored questions of romantic love, commitment, struggle, and ultimately, growth and forgiveness.

was also released in the summer of 2003. These three talented new singers had something else in common aside from their simultaneous successes—all three had been contestants on the hit reality TV show *American Idol*. This fact did not escape Jennifer's attention as she considered her future after *Hercules: The Musical*.

A Balancing Act

When Jennifer's first contract with the Disney Cruise Line expired, the company offered her a second. However, in what turned out to be a monumental career move, Jennifer made a different choice: she turned down the second contract with Disney to try out for the biggest talent competition in the country: *American Idol*.

It was actually Jennifer's mother who first suggested that she try out for *Idol*. Darnell knew the show would give Jennifer more exposure than she had achieved so far and could open her up to a significantly bigger audience than the cruise ship. Jennifer was eager for the opportunity to sing on national television, which would provide a platform for her to show off her extraordinary talent. Even more exciting, the winner of the competition would get a recording contract with a major label—something Jennifer had dreamed of since she was a little girl, listening to Aretha Franklin, Gladys Knight, and other great singers with her grandmother.

Jennifer's experiences in *Big River* and on the Disney cruise ship, as well as all her previous singing gigs in clubs and for church and social functions, had helped her to hone a powerful six-octave singing voice. This amazing vocal range—the ability to sing notes from the lowest (called chest notes) to the highest (called whistle notes)—is extremely rare. In addition, by this time, she had several years of professional experience singing in front of live audiences and had developed a charming and charismatic stage presence. Jennifer Hudson believed she had what it took to become the next *American Idol* winner. As she told an interviewer, if she could keep her balance and composure while performing on the *Disney Wonder* all those months, that proved something about her stamina and determination: "If I can get through the ship, that means I'm cut out for *Idol*."[19]

Chapter **Three**

▼

An American Idol

Jennifer Hudson knew that the winner of the third season of *American Idol* would receive a $1 million recording contract with RCA. However, winning the fierce competition was a serious long shot. At 22 years old, Hudson had only her experience in local theater and on the Disney cruise ship to fall back on. She had no formal training in singing, despite all those hours with her high school choir director and her grandmother. What she had, however, was a powerful voice and a deep determination to pursue a career as a singer. With the encouragement and support of her family, Hudson flew to Atlanta, Georgia, in August 2003 to audition for *American Idol*.

A Once-in-a-Lifetime Chance

Hudson's *American Idol* audition was the first exciting step in a journey that would transform her life. There were 11,000 people auditioning in 6 different cities around the country for the show's third season. When she arrived in Atlanta, some of the thousands of hopefuls there had been waiting outside the Georgia Dome for two days for their big chance. The first hurdle was to sing for the show's producers, who screened contestants before they faced *American Idol's* three judges:

American Idol was the first show of its kind and has shaped every television talent show that has come after it.

Simon Cowell, Paula Abdul, and Randy Jackson. Hudson passed this initial screening and was ready to appear before the judges.

As her audition began, Jackson told her that they expected her to do a better job in the audition than "a cruise ship performance."[20] Hudson, wearing a little black dress for the occasion, assured him she would—and she was true to her word. She then sang "Share Your Love with Me," which was originally recorded by Aretha Franklin. Jackson said of her audition, "Absolutely brilliant, the best singer I've heard so far."[21] Abdul agreed that Hudson's voice was excellent, and Cowell made the decision unanimous. Afterward, Hudson burst through the stage doors singing her announcement to her family that she was going to Hollywood.

The Highs with the Lows

Before reaching Hollywood, however, Hudson had to survive another round of auditions held in Pasadena, California. Hudson flew there with the other 116 contestants from all over the nation who had passed the initial audition. The contestants spent a week practicing and auditioning; only 32 of them would make the cut this time around.

During this round of auditions, Hudson received some criticism from the judges. Cowell, infamous today for being a generally unkind man while judging talent shows, made disparaging comments about her appearance; Abdul and Jackson remained focused on her vocal performance but were critical nonetheless. Although she had wowed them in Atlanta, there was clearly work to be done.

It was not the last time that the judges would negatively critique Hudson, sometimes quite harshly, on both her appearance and the quality of her voice. However, Hudson had a secret weapon: she had known plenty of adversity in her life, and that adversity served only to make her stronger and more determined to achieve her goals. Rather than giving up at the critiques, Hudson reacted by doubling down and working even harder. Cowell's cruel comments did not succeed in humiliating her. As she later explained to journalist Barbara Walters, "If anything, I felt challenged."[22]

Simon Cowell (*center*) gained a reputation for harsh and sometimes rude critiques. He and Hudson had a particularly thorny relationship due to the nature of some of his comments.

One Step Closer

In spite of some pointed criticism, Hudson made it through the auditions in Pasadena to become one of the top 32 contestants who went on to Hollywood. There, she was supported every week by a loving crowd of friends and family, which at various times included her mother, brother, sister, cousins, and boyfriend, James Payton.

As the show progressed week after week, Hudson showed her ability to rise above the judges' sometimes harsh words with grace and style. On the February 10, 2004, broadcast, she had a comeback for Cowell, who had critiqued her wardrobe. After she finished singing "Imagine," which was originally recorded by John Lennon, she jokingly asked Cowell if he liked her outfit that night.

Hudson also endured criticism from Jackson that night. He commented that he "wasn't blown away"[23] by her singing in that round. Hudson took his words in stride, nodding politely. When Abdul observed that Hudson seemed more reserved than usual that night, Hudson replied that she was feeling quite emotional. As she spoke, she was moved to tears, which visibly touched the judges. Later, in the Red Room, where the contestants were interviewed after performing, Hudson told host Ryan Seacrest that she was so emotional because she felt overjoyed to be on the show. She explained, "My dream has always been for the world to hear me sing one time, and this was the second or third, so this is an unbelievable blessing."[24]

Unfortunately for Hudson, in spite of the judges' generally positive response to her performance that night, she was eliminated. The judges did not think her singing was good enough for her to continue, and they voted her off the show during the semifinals. She returned to Chicago with her mother and sister, who had been in the audience watching her perform that night. However, it would not be the last time that America would hear her sing.

A Second Chance

It seemed like this would be the end of Hudson's time on the show, but *American Idol* had other plans. She was invited back to the show for the wild card round. In this round, eight contestants who were eliminated earlier would be brought back for a chance to become a finalist on the show. The three judges

The Original Three

American Idol has featured a variety of judges over the years, but three are most closely identified with the show: Randy Jackson, Paula Abdul, and Simon Cowell.

Jackson is a former session singer and bassist who has recorded with several prominent artists, including Carlos Santana, Aretha Franklin, and Madonna. He is also a record producer and music manager who has worked with Mariah Carey, Whitney Houston, Fergie, and others.

Former Los Angeles Lakers cheerleader Paula Abdul started out in show business as a choreographer, most notably for Janet Jackson. In 1988, Abdul released an album of her own titled *Forever Your Girl*, which produced four number one hit singles. Two more albums followed: the triple platinum *Spellbound* in 1991 and her final album, *Head Over Heels*, in 1995.

British-born Simon Cowell got his start in the mailroom of EMI Music Publishing before becoming a successful music manager and executive. Cowell is best known for his harsh, often rude commentary and for being the cocreator of British-Irish boyband One Direction.

None of the original three judges remain on the show, which, as of 2019, is judged by Katy Perry, Luke Bryan, and Lionel Richie. Ryan Seacrest, who has been the show's host since its premiere in 2002, remains.

would pick one contestant each, and the viewers would choose a fourth. These four would join the remaining eight original contestants to make twelve finalists in all.

Hudson knew this was her last chance on the show and wanted to give an unforgettable performance. During the wild

Hudson got something that not many people do, a second chance at winning *American Idol,* thanks to the wild card round during her season.

card round, broadcast on March 9, 2004, she was the last singer to perform, singing Whitney Houston's "I Believe in You and Me." It is an ambitious song, requiring expert vocal control and a wide range. Her rendition garnered a mixed reaction from the judges—Jackson told her it was the best performance that night, but Cowell thought she needed to improve her vocal control. (In typical fashion, Cowell also called her outfit "hideous."[25]) However, Abdul had only good things to say, and she paid a compliment that meant a lot to Hudson: "You have this muscle in your voice that you flex, and you tell a story with the song. You convey a story and it moves and touches every single one of us."[26]

When the time came for the judges to announce their wild card choices, Jackson spoke first, keeping the contestants in suspense while he explained his thought processes, looking at the performance from the perspective of a producer in the business and as a judge. At last, he announced that his choice for wild card was Jennifer Hudson. She was overjoyed to be brought back to the show as a finalist, yet even at that joyous moment, she was handed a bitter reminder that her vocal talent was not enough: In a world constantly policing women's bodies and appearance, the music business would never simply let her sing. Cowell told her she needed to find a stylist she could see, a reference to her bushy hair that partially covered her eyes.

"Everything About You Is Too Much"

Hudson was at last one of the final 12 contestants. From there on out, her fate—and that of the other contestants—would be decided purely by votes from the reality show's viewers, rather than the judges. Each night the show aired, viewers called a toll-free number to vote for their favorite performer; the performer with the fewest votes after each show would be eliminated one by one.

The competition became sharper and much more demanding. Singing with a flair for the dramatic, which had been an asset when Hudson sang in establishments like drag bars that celebrate over-the-top performance, became a point of critique. After her performance of "Baby, I Love You," which had been made popular by Aretha Franklin, Cowell warned Hudson that if she did not stop oversinging (when a singer pushes her voice too far and winds up off-key), viewers would tire of her. However, when Hudson tried to follow this advice, she was criticized for not being dramatic enough. Another night, Abdul complained that Hudson seemed to be holding back in her performance. It seemed that she simply could not satisfy everyone. As she later told an interviewer, "The *Idol* judges told me, 'Everything about you is too much … Your voice is too much. Your look is too much. Your hair is too much.' I didn't understand. Isn't that what a star is: bigger than average?"[27]

It was not only the *Idol* judges that offered Hudson such criticism. Feedback from viewers on her performances came in the form of low votes during several shows. In fact, during one show, Hudson was in the bottom two. The other contestant in the bottom two, Leah LaBelle, was the one eliminated that night, but it had been a close call for Hudson. Negative comments about her fashion sense appeared in newspapers, magazines, and online chat rooms as well. In later years, Hudson would look back and muse, "At that time I didn't really understand the language of fashion."[28] However, none of the male contestants received this type of obsessive criticism. What's more, Hudson received focused attention on her hair, which at the time she wore in loose, full-body curls. The history of negative stereotypes and devaluation of black hair is long and complex, and while a television talent show is perhaps not the right platform to address the issue, it is difficult not to see troubling echoes in the criticisms Hudson received. Responding to the criticism, Hudson got a makeover from the *Idol* makeup department, and part of this was a sleeking-down of her hair.

During these rounds of the show, Hudson earned a nickname that included two other contestants, Fantasia Barrino and LaToya London. Together, the three women, all of whom are black and have similar voices and singing styles, became known as the "three divas." Because the term "diva" is often applied to a person who is talented but also conceited and demanding, Hudson did not care for the nickname. However, she tried to view it as a compliment that brought her and the other two women a lot of

Hudson's style developed dramatically over the course of her time on *American Idol*, due in part to criticism from the judges.

positive attention, rather than seeing the nickname as an insult.

"You're My American Idol"

By round four of the finals, the contestants had been narrowed down to the final nine. That week's show featured the music of singer and songwriter Elton John, who spent the entire week rehearsing with the contestants. Hudson chose to sing "Circle of Life" from the Disney animated movie *The Lion King*. After one rehearsal of the song, John said that Hudson had an astonishing voice and that listening to her sing gave him chills.

Her performance was a triumph for Hudson, finally silencing her many critics. The judges uniformly praised Hudson after she hit her last note during the live show. Jackson said it was the best performance of the night, as well as the best performance Hudson had given during the season. Abdul complimented Hudson for no longer holding back and for letting her true self shine through. Speaking last, Cowell told her that with that night's performance, she had finally proved that she deserved to be a finalist. It seemed that the harsh criticism was behind her.

In many ways, this song marked a corner turned for Hudson. In round six of the finals, the show was to feature the music of singer and songwriter Barry Manilow, who also spent a week rehearsing with contestants. Hudson performed Manilow's "Weekend in New England." During rehearsals, Manilow commented that Hudson's singing was so good that "it goes to another place."[29] After her performance on the April 21 show, Jackson told her, "That was unbelievable—you just get better every week."[30] The other two judges also raved about her performance.

With all that high praise of her performance, it came as a complete shock when Hudson finished in the bottom three that night, along with London and Barrino. Then, it was revealed that Hudson had received the fewest number of call-in votes. She was eliminated from the show, finishing in seventh place.

The studio audience, the contestants, and even the judges were shocked by the announcement. Hudson looked numb. The studio audience remained silent, and some of the contestants began to cry. Fantasia Barrino threw her arms around Hudson and

The 3Ds

After Jennifer Hudson was voted off *American Idol*, two of the "three divas" still remained: LaToya London and Fantasia Barrino. Both women would go on to achieve success after leaving *Idol*. Fourth-place-finisher London released her debut album, *Love & Life*, in September 2005. The album, a mix of rhythm and blues, soul, jazz, and hip-hop, was not a commercial success. However, London found success on the stage. From 2007 to 2010, she earned rave reviews for her performance in the national tour of the Broadway musical *The Color Purple*. In 2010, she formed Urban Punk with hip-hop artist H2O.

Season Three winner Fantasia released her debut album, *Free Yourself*, in November 2004. The album earned her four Grammy nominations. In 2006, she released her second album, *Fantasia*, which received three Grammy nominations. She was nominated for yet another Grammy for her duet with Jennifer Hudson, titled "I'm His Only Woman." The year 2010 saw the release of *Back to Me*, a commercial success, and then, in 2016, *The Definition Of ...* topped the R&B/Hip-Hip Album chart. In March 2019, Fantasia announced that she had finished her sixth album but did not give a release date or title. On May 1 of that same year, she released the lead single, "Enough." She was inducted into the North Carolina Music Hall of Fame in 2014.

proclaimed in a voice choked with emotion, "You are my American Idol!"[31] Fantasia—who went on to win that season—later revealed that she was upset by the outcome of that night's vote: "I was really angry when she got voted off."[32]

Race, Music, and the American Public

Hudson's final elimination was the result of one of the closest votes in the show's history, and it sparked a controversy over

Elton John is a singer, songwriter, pianist, and composer, and he is one of the most popular musicians in the world.

the show's voting system. Elton John called that night's voting "incredibly racist."[33] He went on to explain that three of the performers he thought were very talented—and who also happened to be black—kept finishing in the bottom three in the voting. It was not only John who made this observation. The *New York Post*, which was owned by the same company that owned Fox, the network on with *American Idol* aired, was flooded with calls from people who wanted the paper to investigate complaints of racially motivated voting.

A few other theories circulated for why the votes turned out the way they did that night. One theory is based on the fact that there was a series of windstorms and tornadoes that night in the area around Chicago—Hudson's hometown—and 15,000 homes lost power and telephone service. It was possible, Hudson fans suggested, that thousands of people in Chicago who could have been trying to call in to vote for Hudson were unable to get through. Another theory is that Hudson, Barrino, and London were simply the victims of the phenomenon known as vote splitting: Because these three contestants were so similar, callers who liked that singing style best split their votes three ways, with the result that not one of the three got a clear majority of votes. This idea helps explain why the three women kept receiving a low number of votes.

After Hudson's elimination, there were calls to change the way the show's voting was handled. Some people wanted the network to make the results of the voting public so that the number of votes received by each contestant was clear. Others proposed the network find a way to limit the number of times that a person could call in and vote. However, the controversy over the show's voting system did not change anything for Hudson; she left *American Idol* and headed back to Chicago.

Strength in Adversity

Despite coming in seventh place, Hudson's appearance on *American Idol* had drawn national attention. She remained calm and focused after her elimination, as she explained later: "I just knew I was going somewhere and I had to sing my way to it. And

I couldn't give up."[34] She remained grateful for the experience and the exposure that *American Idol* brought her. She knew that even without winning, the show could be a launchpad for her career and could lead her on to bigger and better opportunities—but even she could not have imagined what was waiting for her on the horizon.

Immediately after her final elimination, she made several TV appearances. She went on *Entertainment Tonight* and several talk shows. She also appeared on *The Late Show with David Letterman* and read "The Top 10 Things I Can Say Now That I've Lost *American Idol*." A compilation CD titled *American Idol Season 3: Greatest Soul Classics*, which included one song from each of the twelve finalists, was released in the spring of 2004. Hudson contributed the song "Neither One of Us (Wants to Be the First to Say Goodbye)," made popular by Gladys Knight and the Pips. Hudson also toured the United States with the American Idol Live! tour in the summer of 2004, singing songs by Aretha Franklin, Prince, and Beyoncé. At the end of the tour, Hudson returned home, where she was very much sought after as a performer around Chicago.

Her experiences on *American Idol* taught Hudson the importance of hard work and perseverance, lessons that would come in handy as she continued her professional journey. As for being eliminated from the show, Hudson had some words of advice for future *Idol* contestants. She cautioned them not to let criticism get to them and also not to let anyone intimidate them. "Believe in yourself and know that you are a star,"[35] Hudson said. It is perhaps this attitude that helped her to remain strong through all the ups and downs of her experience on *American Idol* and to not let her final elimination discourage her from pursuing a career as a singer.

Dream, Work, Do

Hudson knew that, despite the painful and public rejection of her exit from *American Idol*, her career was only just beginning. She had always been hardworking and ambitious, and in many ways *Idol* was always only meant to be a launching pad for her to achieve far greater things than winning a talent show, even one that was on nationally broadcast television.

After returning to her hometown of Chicago after the conclusion of the American Idol Live! tour, she hoped to leverage her involvement in that project to attract interest from record labels, but nothing materialized. To keep working while she planned her next move, Hudson returned to singing at weddings and nightclubs around the city, and although this felt like a step back after her turn on television's most popular reality show, she kept her eyes open for opportunities to move forward.

Her first chance was a role in 2004's Broadway production of *Hair*, a rock musical that at the time was also starring television personalities like Wayne Brady, RuPaul, and Michael McKean. Although the show was only a one-night performance, produced by the Actors Fund of America toward its mission to provide aid to entertainment professionals, it gave her the chance to get out of Chicago and mix with other

Hudson performed on tour with her *American Idol* castmates after the conclusion of the season.

entertainers. It also gave her a gift that would come in handy later: "Easy to Be Hard," her song in the show.

Determined not to miss her moment, and without any offers for a recording contract, Hudson decided to produce an album on her own. She spent about a year on the project before something happened that would radically change her life forever: Hudson saw a casting call.

Jennifer Hudson and Effie White

The movie that caught Hudson's eye was called *Dreamgirls*, the film adaptation of the hit Broadway musical of the same name. The musical opened on Broadway in 1981 and ran for more than 1,500 performances, picking up six Tony Awards along the way. *Dreamgirls* was adapted for the screen by screenwriter and director Bill Condon, and it tells the story of the rise of an all-girl singing group called the Dreamettes in the 1960s and 1970s. The Dreamettes were a fictional group, but their story is closely based on the real-life all-girl group the Supremes.

Hudson decided to audition for the part of Effie White, who begins the show as the talented but difficult lead singer of the Dreamettes and is eventually replaced by a singer with a weaker voice but who is slimmer and easier for their manager to control. It would be a major role requiring a performer who could act alongside some of Hollywood's biggest stars and sing alongside powerhouse vocalists like Beyoncé. Although the 25-year-old Hudson had experience from her turns in *Big River*, *Hercules*, and *Hair*, those roles had been primarily singing parts, with only one or two lines of speaking. *Dreamgirls* would demand the performance of a lifetime. Despite the ambitious nature of the project, Hudson was determined to win the role of Effie and prove she could act as well as sing.

She was up against very stiff competition for the role. There were 782 women auditioning for the part—including *American Idol* winner Fantasia Barrino. For her audition, Hudson sang "Easy to Be Hard," which she had performed in *Hair*. Then, she had to wait three months to find out whether she would be called back for a second audition. Time passed slowly while she waited.

Effie White in Real Life

Dreamgirls' Effie White is based on a real-life singer named Florence Ballard. Along with childhood friends Diana Ross and Mary Wilson, the Detroit-born Ballard formed a group called the Supremes, who would go on to be one of the most successful girl groups of the 1960s. In 1964, the three women signed a deal with Motown Records. Originally, Ballard was considered the lead singer, but she was gradually replaced in this role by Ross, whom the record producers thought was prettier and more likely to appeal to white audiences than Ballard. In 1967, the group's name was changed to Diana Ross and the Supremes, after which Ballard began missing public appearances and recording sessions. She was soon fired. Her attempt at a solo career in the late 1960s was unsuccessful, and she sank into a spiral of alcohol, poverty, and depression. Ballard remained largely forgotten by the public until a story about her misfortunes appeared in national newspapers in 1974. She enjoyed a brief comeback before her sudden death in 1976 from a blood clot near her heart. Hudson mentioned Ballard when accepting a Golden Globe for *Dreamgirls*, saying, "I want to dedicate this award to a lady who never got a fair chance, Florence Ballard. You will never be forgotten."[1]

1. Jennifer Hudson acceptance speech, *64th Annual Golden Globe Awards*, NBC, January 15, 2007.

Hudson had nearly given up on hearing back from the producers when a casting agent called and asked her to read for the part in person. Much like the audition for *American Idol*, the casting process for *Dreamgirls* would be an emotional roller coaster for Hudson. The movie's director and producers were concerned

For Jennifer Hudson, Effie White would be the role of a lifetime.

about her lack of acting experience, and this showed in their hesitation to cast her. Despite her inexperience, though, Hudson clearly had a spark in her, and they could not let her walk away either. Over the next six months, Hudson auditioned two more times in New York. During this time, she received extremely mixed messages from those in charge. Sometimes she felt that she was a shoo-in for the part, and others she was told that she had already lost the race. At long last, she was asked to do a screen test in Los Angeles, California, and two days later, Condon called to tell her that the role of Effie White was hers.

Effie White was the role of a lifetime for Hudson. The production already had a big-name cast that included Jamie Foxx, Eddie Murphy, Danny Glover, and Anika Noni Rose. Perhaps most exciting of all, the movie starred one of Hudson's favorite singers and her personal idol, Beyoncé. Hudson's involvement in the project as one of its stars would mean an extraordinary amount of exposure and the opportunity to showcase her talent in a forum completely different from any other she had experience with so far.

Life was about to change dramatically for Jennifer Hudson.

A Star Is Born

When *Dreamgirls* premiered in December 2006, moviegoers were immediately taken with Hudson's debut performance. She had an easy, natural acting ability, and viewers identified with the raw emotion and vulnerability she conveyed in her portrayal of Effie. So powerful was her rendition of the six-octave "And I Am Telling You I'm Not Going" that audiences could not contain their enthusiasm for her performance. "It's not often that a movie audience breaks into spontaneous applause,"[36] points out movie critic Roger Ebert, yet that is exactly what happened in theaters across America.

In his review of the movie, Peter Travers of *Rolling Stone* magazine referred to Hudson as "a blazing new star." Travers added, "She can act ... and she can sing until the roof comes off the multiplex."[37] Viewers and critics alike thought that Hudson had outperformed pop star Beyoncé. During a guest appearance on

Hudson won an Academy Award for Best Supporting Actress for her first major role.

The Late Show with David Letterman, Letterman said to Hudson: "They put you in this movie, which is a wonderful story, and incredibly talented people, and you come in and you steal the whole movie—your first time out!"[38]

Hudson's performance in *Dreamgirls* garnered her a total of 36 award nominations. Of these, she won 30. Her awards as best supporting actress include a Golden Globe Award, a BAFTA Award, an NAACP Image Award, and a Screen Actors Guild Award. Then, she was nominated for the most prestigious of all awards, the Academy Award, or Oscar, for Best Supporting Actress.

Hudson went on to win the Oscar, becoming one of only a handful of actors to win the award for a debut screen performance. With her mother in the audience the night of the awards show, Hudson gave an emotional acceptance speech. "Oh my God, I have to just take this moment in," she said through tears. "I cannot believe this. Look what God can do. I didn't think I was going to win. If my grandmother was here to see me now. She was my biggest inspiration."[39] Hudson ended her acceptance speech by thanking Jennifer Holliday, the Tony Award–winning actress who had originally played the role of Effie White on Broadway.

An Overnight Success

In addition to the numerous acting awards, Hudson received attention for her version of the song "And I Am Telling You I'm Not Going." The song was released as a single, debuting at number 98 on the Billboard Hot 100 in January 2007. One month later, the song became a top 10 hit on the Billboard Hot Adult R&B Airplay chart. It also reached number 14 on the Billboard Hot R&B/Hip-Hop Songs chart.

The song had another benefit for Hudson as well. After music industry executive Clive Davis saw Hudson's screen test for the movie, in which she sang "And I Am Telling You I'm Not Going," he immediately offered her a contract with Arista Records. Davis is a legendary record producer who worked with artists such as Kelly Clarkson, Alicia Keys, Carlos Santana, Barry Manilow, and another of Hudson's personal idols, Whitney Houston.

In September 2008, Hudson released her debut album, *Jennifer Hudson*. The self-titled album, which debuted at number two on the Billboard 200 chart, was a collection of soul, rhythm and blues, and pop. The first single, a ballad titled "Spotlight," went to number one on the Billboard Hot R&B/Hip-Hop Songs chart. In all, the successful album produced five singles and three music videos. *Jennifer Hudson*, which sold more than 800,000 copies worldwide, was certified gold by the Recording Industry Association of America. It was also nominated for four Grammy Awards and won the Grammy for best rhythm and blues album.

Finding Her Way

Hudson's tremendous success in *Dreamgirls*, as well as the success of her debut album, helped kick her career into high gear. In the months following the movie's release, she made numerous TV appearances, including interviews on *Oprah* and *The Late Show with David Letterman*. She also appeared on the covers of several magazines, and in 2007, she became the first African American singer and only the third African American celebrity to appear on the cover of *Vogue* (after Halle Berry and Oprah Winfrey).

In 2008, the same year her album was released, Hudson appeared in two other movies, neither of which revolved around singing. The first of these was *Sex and the City*, in 2008. The movie was based on the hit HBO TV series that ran from 1998 to 2004, which in turn, was based on the novel *Sex and the City* by Candace Bushnell. Hudson played the part of Louise, the assistant to Carrie Bradshaw, who was played by Sarah Jessica Parker both on TV and in the movie. Hudson also sang the song "All Dressed in Love" on the movie's soundtrack, which debuted at number two on the Billboard 200. The movie was a financial success, becoming the year's top-grossing romantic comedy.

Sex and the City garnered mixed reviews from critics. A reviewer for the *New York Times* referred to it as "vulgar, shrill, deeply shallow."[40] Several publications, including the *London Times*, the *Daily Telegraph*, and the *New York Observer*, featured *Sex and the City* on their list of the year's worst movies. A reviewer for *Newsweek*, however, called the movie "incredibly sweet and touching,"[41] and the *Los Angeles Times* called Hudson's performance as Louise "likeable."[42]

Hudson's second film of 2008 was *The Secret Life of Bees*, which costarred Queen Latifah, Alicia Keys, and Dakota Fanning. The movie, about the lives of a group of black women and one white child in the South during the 1960s, was adapted from the novel of the same name by Sue Monk Kidd. Hudson played the character of Rosaleen, who is beaten and arrested while trying to vote in a South Carolina town. Like *Sex and the City*, *The Secret Life of Bees* received mixed reviews. A. O. Scott of the *New York Times* said it was "a familiar and tired fable."[43] Roger Ebert found it an unrealistic and inaccurate portrayal of life in the South during the civil rights era but called it "enchanting"[44] nonetheless. The movie review website Rotten Tomatoes echoed Ebert's sentiments with its report: "*The Secret Life of Bees* has moments of charm, but is largely too maudlin and sticky-sweet."[45] Although reviewers did not single out Hudson, she did receive a nomination for an NAACP Award for Outstanding Supporting Actress in a Motion Picture for her performance in the movie.

One of the biggest honors Hudson received during this time came on August 28, 2008, at the Democratic National Convention in Denver, Colorado. She was invited by a fellow Chicagoan, Illinois senator Barack Obama, who at the time was campaigning for the presidency, to sing the national anthem on the last day of the convention. Her stirring performance of "The Star-Spangled Banner" at Invesco Field was broadcast live on national television.

An End and a Beginning

Hudson had experienced incredible changes in her professional life in just a few short years. She had gone from being sent home twice from *American Idol* to one of the biggest names in show business. Her work life was not the only thing changing. During this time, major changes occurred in her personal life as well. She and James Payton, who had been dating for seven years when Hudson won her Oscar, faced a host of changes. Now that she was a big star, many wondered whether the romance would last. Barbara Walters suggested as much when she interviewed

Queen Latifah: Rapper, Singer, Actress

The rapper, actress, and singer known as Queen Latifah, who costarred in *The Secret Life of Bees* along with Jennifer Hudson, was born Dana Elaine Owens in Newark, New Jersey, in 1970. She first gained attention as a hip-hop artist when her debut album, *All Hail the Queen*, was released in 1989. The album reached number six on the Billboard Top R&B/Hip-Hop Albums chart. In 1995, Latifah won a Grammy Award for Best Solo Rap Performance for her single "U.N.I.T.Y." She has received six other Grammy nominations and is largely hailed as among the best female rappers of all time. Latifah has also been recognized for her work as a pioneer feminist and voice for women in hip-hop.

Latifah starred in her own sitcom, *Living Single*, on Fox from 1993 to 1998. She also had her own talk show, *The Queen Latifah Show*, from 2013 to 2015. Her performance in the 2002 film *Chicago* earned her an Oscar nomination for Best Supporting Actress. Her film career blossomed after this, and in 2015, she coproduced the HBO film *Bessie*, which won a Primetime Emmy Award for Outstanding Television Movie. She has a star on the Hollywood Walk of Fame, a Grammy, an Emmy, a Golden Globe, three Screen Actors Guild Awards, two NAACP Image Awards, and an Academy Award nomination as of 2019.

Hudson on her traditional Oscar show: "Jennifer, realistically, James is a maintenance engineer in Chicago. Now you've got Hollywood, you're going to London, you're going to Paris, there's stuff, there's things. It changes relationships sometimes, doesn't

The versatile performer also has her own line of cosmetics, designed specifically for women of color, in partnership with CoverGirl called CoverGirl Queen. She also has a perfume line called Queen. In addition, she has sold nearly 2 million records worldwide.

Queen Latifah is known as one of the best female rappers of all time.

it?"[46] Hudson replied to Walters's observation, "We are happy with the place we are right now, but perhaps we will tie the knot someday."[47] Despite Hudson's hopeful outlook, in late 2007, the couple split ways.

Hudson began dating David Otunga after her relationship with James Payton ended.

It was the end of a chapter for Hudson, who had been dating Payton since her early days struggling to make her music career take off, but it was also the beginning of a new phase in her life. Her career was blossoming, the accolades were pouring in, and that spring, she met David Otunga, a graduate of the University of Illinois and of Harvard Law School and a WWE wrestler and commentator. Otunga was also a reality TV actor who had appeared as a contestant nicknamed Punk on the VH1 show *I Love New York 2*, a reality dating show. Otunga and Hudson met in May 2008 and soon began dating. He accompanied her to several promotional events for her movies and upcoming album, and he was in the audience, alongside Hudson's mother, for her performance at the Democratic National Convention.

Seven months after the couple met, Otunga planned a surprise for Hudson. He took her to a beach near Los Angeles on her 27th birthday, September 12, 2008. There, he had a picnic laid out for her. Later, he handed her a plastic shovel and told her a present was buried in the sand. As she dug, she found card after card from him declaring his love for her. When she turned to face him, he dropped down on one knee and asked her to marry him. Hudson tearfully said yes, though the couple did not set a wedding date at that time.

Everything seemed to be going Hudson's way in the fall of 2008. With a diamond-and-platinum engagement ring on her finger, a recently released album, and her latest movie, *The Secret Life of Bees*, opening in October of that year, her career and personal life were going strong. However, within a few short days of the release of that film, an unthinkable tragedy threatened to derail everything for Hudson.

Hard to Say Goodbye

There is no one on earth who lives without experiencing both joy and sorrow; this is just as true for celebrities as for people whose accomplishments go uncelebrated. On Friday, October 24, 2008, Jennifer Hudson was still riding the crest of an incredible wave of success and celebration. She was newly engaged, she had a film in theaters across America, and her debut album had already sold nearly half a million copies despite being released just a month before. She and her fiancé were planning a trip to Los Angeles, where she was scheduled to receive an award alongside the rest of *The Secret Life of Bees* cast.

However, life had other plans.

An Unthinkable Tragedy

On October 24, at 3:00 p.m., Jennifer's sister, Julia, returned from work to the family home on South Yale Avenue on Chicago's South Side. What she found was not the warm, welcoming place she had left that morning. Instead, the Hudson family home had been stained with violence: A family member had found the body of the Hudson family matriarch. Darnell, who had provided her children with support, with love, and with guidance, now lay on the living room floor. She had been shot to death.

Hudson was enjoying the success of *The Secret Life of Bees* when her life was shaken by tragedy.

The tragedy of that afternoon had not finished playing out. When the police arrived, they discovered the body of Jason Hudson, Jennifer and Julia's brother, in a bedroom. Just 29, Jason, too, had been shot to death. There was no one else in the house, even though Julia's seven-year-old son with Gregory King, Julian, had been home from school that day because of teacher meetings. Police searched the entire property, but there was no sign of the second-grader.

Mystifyingly, there was also no sign of forced entry. Investigators believed the shooter had fired through a door and struck Jason first, then entered the house and continued to shoot, hitting

In the wake of the tragedy, Hudson and her family received love and support from their friends and neighbors.

Jason's mother when she ran into the living room. The slayings were believed to have occurred between 8:00 and 9:00 that morning. Neighbors had heard shots ring out, but gunfire was so common in the neighborhood that no one had bothered to call 911. This allowed the killer a six- to seven-hour head start before the discovery of the bodies.

The authorities issued an AMBER Alert (a child abduction alert) for Julian King early that evening. Included in the alert was the boy's stepfather, 27-year-old William Balfour, who was also missing and was considered a suspect. Balfour, Julia's estranged husband, was an ex-convict who had served nearly seven years in prison for carjacking and attempted murder. He had missed a meeting with his parole officer early in the afternoon on the day of the slayings. The parole officer reached Balfour on his cell phone, and Balfour told the officer he was babysitting on the West Side. The parole officer later reported that he heard a child's voice in the background.

Shortly after the AMBER Alert was issued, police tracked Balfour through his cell phone records to his girlfriend's apartment on the West Side. Balfour was arrested, but Julian was not with him. There was also no sign of Jason Hudson's white SUV, which was missing from the Hudsons' home. The police suspected that Balfour had taken Julian away from the home in the car.

Waiting in Hope

Jennifer Hudson immediately flew to Chicago from Florida when she learned what had happened. She was given the difficult task of identifying the bodies of her mother and brother at the morgue late that night. The double murder was horrifying, but Jennifer and the rest of the family held out hope that little Julian was still alive. In the morning, the FBI was called in to search for the missing child, since authorities believed he may have been taken out of state. Detectives worked around the clock. Dozens of officers joined family and friends in searching for the boy or for information as to his whereabouts.

Despite multiple searches of the Hudson home and surrounding area, Julian remained missing. However, police did recover

Gun Violence in America

The national conversation around gun violence in America has gotten much louder over the course of the last decade, most notably after the Marjory Stoneman Douglas High School shooting in 2018. It is a complex issue, but the facts are clear. Every day, 100 Americans are killed with guns; in an average month, 52 American women are shot to death by a romantic partner. Guns are the second-leading cause of death for American children and teens, after car accidents, and 58 percent of American adults or someone they care about have experienced gun violence in their lifetime. Three million American children witness gun violence every year. This is as true in Chicago, and the Englewood neighborhood where the Hudsons lived, as elsewhere in the United States.

Some people argue for better gun control—that is, to reduce the number of gun deaths by reducing the number of guns available by making them more difficult to buy. Some studies suggest that violence of this kind ought to be treated at the neighborhood level, through anti-poverty and community health initiatives, because exposure to violence increases a person's risk of adopting violent behavior themselves.

shell casings, which are pieces of ammunition expelled from a gun when it is reloaded, confirming that shots had been fired in the home. That evening, with Julian missing for nearly 36 hours, Hudson and her family made a public plea, offering a $100,000 reward for his safe return. Hudson also posted this message on her MySpace page: "Thank you all for your prayers and your calls. Please keep praying for our family and that we get Julian King back home safely."[48]

Friends and neighbors gave tremendous support to the grieving, frantic family, helping to comb the area in search of the boy. Angela Russell, a next-door neighbor of the Hudsons, told an interviewer for *The Early Show* on CBS, "There's no words of comfort that anybody can offer at this point. I think the only thing the family really feels will comfort them is having Julian in their arms, knowing that he is safe and okay."[49]

Everyone clung to hopes that Julian would be found alive, but it was not to be. Early in the morning on Monday, October 27, Chicago resident John Louden, who lived only a couple of miles from Balfour's girlfriend, made a chilling discovery outside his home. A white SUV had been parked near Louden's house since noon on Friday. On Monday morning, Louden's dog ran up to the car and began to bark and howl in a way the man had never before heard. Unsettled by his pet's reaction, Louden wrote down the license plate number and returned to his house. His wife had written down the license plate number of the missing Hudson vehicle that was issued in the AMBER Alert bulletins about Julian's disappearance. When they compared the numbers and realized that the SUV was the one police were looking for, Louden called the authorities. Police arrived within two minutes.

What they found was the worst possible outcome of the search for Julian King. The body of the young boy was inside the car, shot in the head. A gun was also found near the car, and police determined that the gun had been used to kill all three victims. Once again, it fell to Jennifer Hudson to identify her loved one at the morgue. She remained calm when she saw Julian's body, saying only, "Yes, that is him."[50]

The Perpetrator Found

Even before Julian had been found, the investigation led police to a suspect, William Balfour, who had moved out of the Hudson family home in May 2008 when he and Julia Hudson separated. At the time of the murders, Balfour was still on parole for a 1999 carjacking and attempted murder conviction.

Investigators in the case believed they had unraveled the reasons behind Balfour's alleged violence. Balfour and Julia Hudson had had several heated arguments in the time period leading up to the murders. One of these arguments concerned Balfour's jealous suspicions that his estranged wife was dating someone new. In addition, acting in a "jealous rage,"[51] he had threatened to take

Domestic Violence in America

Domestic violence is a difficult thing to escape. It can be hard for men and women in abusive relationships to understand what is happening because often abuse does not begin with physical violence—it could start in a variety of other ways, like controlling behavior, stalking, or manipulation, often in the form of gaslighting (when someone makes their partner believe that their experiences are not real or that they are overreacting or misunderstanding what has happened to them to prevent them from reporting it).

Although there are stereotypes that suggest men and women who are unable to leave their partner are weak, statistics show that often they feel unable to leave because of the threat of violence against them or their loved ones or because they do not know where to turn for help. More than one in three women and more than one in four men have experienced intimate partner violence in their lifetime; it affects more than 12 million people in America every year. It is deadly: Nearly half of women who were murdered in the past decade were killed by a current or former intimate partner.

Although she did not attend the public memorial, she did attend a private service held a few days later. The grief-stricken Hudson managed to maintain her composure at the funeral. "Jennifer is the pillar," family friend Glover Lewis commented. "It's obvious she's holding the family together."[54]

Taking Time to Heal

Hudson remained in seclusion for months afterward as she tried to come to grips with the loss of her mother, brother, and nephew. She said later during an interview that she spent two weeks straight inside one room, with only family and friends coming

After the tragedy that changed her life, Hudson took time to herself to heal before returning to the stage.

In Tampa, Florida, in 2009 Hudson, too, would lip-sync, but the track she used was her own rendition, a rendition that was clearly filled with emotion. Those in attendance in the stadium—including some of the football players—were clearly moved. *American Idol* music director Ricky Minor, who has served as the pregame show producer for numerous Super Bowl games and was Houston's creative partner for her 1991 performance, was the producer for Super Bowl XLIII. After Hudson's performance, Minor told the Associated Press that Hudson was in great spirits that day. Then he summed up: "She's on fire right now and totally grounded."[57]

When Hudson returned to her dressing room, she was flooded with support from friends, family, and colleagues, including a text message on her cell phone from *Dreamgirls* costar Jamie Foxx, in which he told her she had brought tears to his eyes. The last months had been a long, dark tunnel, but she had arrived at the light.

Indeed, Hudson threw herself into a whirlwind of public performances after the Super Bowl. She performed at the 51st Grammy Awards ceremony on February 8, 2009, and on the same occasion, received a Grammy for her debut album. This special moment for Hudson was made even more special because the award was presented to her by one of her idols, Whitney Houston, who called Hudson "absolutely one of the greatest voices of our time."[58] Hudson gave a very emotional acceptance speech. When she sang "You Pulled Me Through" from her album, she teared up toward the end. The song took on special meaning in light of what had happened to her family. Ricky Minor said her performance "just reaches straight through the television, just grabs your heart … It was just amazing."[59]

Hudson next appeared at the 40th NAACP Image Awards ceremony, broadcast live from the Shrine Auditorium in Los Angeles on February 12, 2009. She won three awards, including the award for Outstanding New Artist. On this occasion, she gave an emotional performance of the song "The Impossible Dream" as a tribute to boxing legend Muhammad Ali. She also appeared as a guest on the eighth season of *American Idol* the

Hudson's performance at the Super Bowl was applauded by football fans and musicians alike.

following April, and she gave a live performance of "If This Isn't Love," the second single from her album.

Finding Solace in Music

Having successfully stepped back into the spotlight, Hudson threw herself into her music. She gave numerous other public performances as 2009 progressed, including an appearance at an all-star tribute to Neil Diamond in which she sang his 1969 hit "Holly Holy." Hudson received a standing ovation for her performance, and rap-rocker Kid Rock, who performed next, joked backstage afterward, "I'm gonna kill whoever made me follow Jennifer Hudson. Thanks!"[60]

She continued making public appearances that summer and fall, notably at the memorial service for Michael Jackson shortly after his death, singing Jackson's "Will You Be There." (Hudson later performed in the star-studded tribute to Michael Jackson on the 2010 Grammy Awards show.) In September 2009, she performed "Spotlight" for the VH1 Divas concert, which also included Paula Abdul, Sheryl Crow, Cyndi Lauper, Melissa Etheridge, Martina McBride, Leona Lewis, Kelly Clarkson, and Miley Cyrus, among others.

In September 2010, Hudson performed at a concert that was very close to her heart. She celebrated her 29th birthday by performing in a gospel concert at Christ Universal Temple in Chicago. All proceeds from the concert went to the Julian D. King Gift Foundation, which was set up in honor of her late nephew, to provide gifts for children during the holiday season.

Finding Forgiveness

In 2012, Hudson joined Oprah Winfrey for an interview on Winfrey's television network, OWN. Though she was joined for part of the interview by her sister, Julia, Hudson first spoke on her own, delving honestly into what she had gone through during Balfour's trial and as she grieved for her family. Though she admitted that seeing Balfour at the trial "made [her] skin crawl," when asked whether she had forgiven him, Hudson said: "Yes. I feel like, for the most part, it's not his fault. It's what he was taught, how he was brought up … We tried to offer love, but you were so far gone that you didn't even see that. A lot of things came out [during the trial] that we didn't

Hudson has worked with Oprah Winfrey on multiple projects, and it was with Winfrey that Hudson chose to give her most in-depth interview after the tragedy.

know about, from his upbringing, which is like … he never had a chance. You never had a chance. If he'd had the love that my mother gave us … then you would have stood a chance … So how can your heart not go out to that?"[61]

Still, forgiveness or no, Hudson made it clear that she held Balfour responsible for his actions. It was only after he was found guilty that she felt she was able to visit her loved ones' graves because she felt that she had something to offer them: Their killer had been brought to justice.

Life Moves Ahead

On August 10, 2009, the 27-year-old Hudson and her then-fiancé, David Otunga, welcomed their son, David Daniel Otunga

Starting a Foundation

The Julian D. King Gift Foundation was established in 2009 as a way for Jennifer and Julia Hudson to honor their family and find meaning in tragedy. The foundation holds several events throughout the course of the year and focuses on providing "stability, support, and positive experiences for children of all backgrounds to enable them to grow up to be productive, confident, and happy adults."[1] The organization focuses in part on providing school supplies and Christmas presents to those who need them across Chicago, but it also hosts a yearly Hatch Day, on August 14, which was Julian's birthday. Hatch Day is what Julian used to call his birthday, something he had taken from a cartoon he loved. It has become one of the largest charitable events in the Chicagoland area and is an opportunity for the foundation to serve the city's children in honor of Julian's memory.

1. "About Us," Julian D. King Gift Foundation, accessed on June 17, 2018. www.juliandkinggiftfoundation.com/about-us/.

Jr., into the world. Though her relationship with Otunga would not last (they split in 2017) and the separation would result in a difficult custody battle over their son, Hudson has adored being a mother and has said that in the wake of her mother's loss, her relationship with her son kept her going, saying, "I tell David ... all the time, 'You saved my life.'"[62] She also finds comfort in the new life she was able to bring into the world after losing three of her family members and said, "Being a mother reminds me of my mom ... I want him to get the same love and the same upbringing as my mother gave us, and I know for sure that way he'll be loved."[63]

Hudson also continued to build on her professional success. In 2011, she released her second album, *I Remember Me*.

Every year, the Julian D. King Gift Foundation celebrates Hatch Day by giving students in Chicago school supplies and gifts.

She played a larger role in the creative direction of this album and hoped that it would be a celebratory project. *I Remember Me* was well-received critically, debuting at number 2 on the U.S. Billboard 200. It was certified gold by the Recording Industry Association of America. In 2014, she released *JHUD*, which also met with success: Hudson was nominated for a Grammy for Best R&B Performance for the single "It's Your World." The feel and flow of *JHUD* was a further evolution of Hudson's sound; it debuted at number 10 on the U.S. Billboard 200 chart and number two on the Top R&B/Hip-Hop Albums chart.

Getting Back into the Groove

Although Hudson will likely always be a musician above all, in recent years, she has continued to explore and grow her acting talents. In 2011, she starred in a biopic (a movie about the life of a real person) about Winnie Mandela, a controversial figure in South African history, and in 2012, she had a part in *The Three Stooges*. She also delved back into television, appearing on NBC's *Smash* in 2013 and Fox's *Empire*. Her character on *Empire*, named Michelle White, is a music therapist and gospel singer who is used as a pawn by the devious Lucious Lyon, played by Terrence Howard.

Not content to simply stay in her comfort zone, Hudson joined the Broadway revival of *The Color Purple*, portraying Shug Avery. *The Color Purple* explores the lives of African American women in the South in the 1930s and does not shy away from the difficulties that they faced. Hudson's character, Shug, is a blues singer who befriends the main character, Celie, and helps her find hope despite her dark world. Hudson won another Grammy for her work on the musical. Then, in 2016, Hudson joined NBC's *Hairspray Live!* playing the role of Motormouth Maybelle, who was played by Queen Latifah in the 2007 film version of the popular musical about life in Baltimore, Maryland, in the 1960s. She also performed in 2016's animated musical *Sing*, lending her voice to "Golden Slumbers/Carry That Weight" for the film

Hairspray! Live was broadcast on NBC, and Hudson's performance received praise.

Using Her Voice to Protest Gun Violence

After the tragedy that affected her family, Hudson became a passionate advocate against gun violence in America. On March 24, 2018, she joined hundreds of thousands of people to demonstrate support for legislative action to prevent gun violence in the wake of the mass shooting at Marjory Stoneman Douglas High School in Parkland, Florida. Hudson closed out the March for Our Lives rally with a performance of Bob Dylan's protest song, "The Times They Are A-Changin'."

Hudson had already been lending her voice to the gun violence prevention movement. In an interview with *W Magazine* in 2015, she criticized the idea that gun violence was primarily an issue in certain cities. "It's not just the city of Chicago. It's everywhere,"[1] she said.

At the March for Our Lives rally, Hudson joined other celebrities in spreading the message that it was time to make change. Speaking to the crowd, she reflected on her own journey and the journey of the Parkland students who had organized the rally, saying, "We've all lost somebody. We all got a purpose, and we all want change."[2]

1. Quoted in Vanessa Lawrence, "Jennifer Hudson Sounds Off on Gun Control," *W Magazine*, December 9, 2015. www.wmagazine.com/story/jennifer-hudson-color-purple.

2. Quoted in Dave Quinn, "Jennifer Hudson Closes March for Our Lives with Emotional Performance After Losing Family to Gun Violence," PEOPLE.com, March 24, 2018. people.com/music/march-for-our-lives-jennifer-hudson-closes-dc-protest/.

as well as partnering with Tori Kelly to sing "Hallelujah" on the soundtrack.

Later that same year, she signed with Epic Records. Famous producer Clive Davis said of the signing, "I signed Jennifer ... believing her to be the strongest candidate as the next genera-

Hudson's personal experience with gun violence inspired her performance during the March for Our Lives in 2018.

tion's Aretha Franklin and Whitney [Houston]. She has become that."[64] Although there has been no new album from the signing as of summer 2019, Hudson has released two singles: "Burden Down" and "Remember Me." The lyrics for both songs explore hardship in Hudson's life, perhaps referencing her split

Notes

Introduction: Sweet Home Chicago

1. Jennifer Hudson, interview by David Letterman, *The Late Show with David Letterman*, CBS, January 8, 2007.

2. Quoted in Maudlyne Ihejirika, "Jennifer Hudson at Women's Conference: 'We Have No Choice but to Keep On Going,'" *Chicago Sun Times*, September 1, 2018. chicago.suntimes.com/entertainment/jennifer-hudson-womens-conference-murder-aretha-franklin.

3. Quoted in *Access Hollywood*, "Jennifer Hudson: The Girl Behind the 'Dream,'" December 17, 2006.www.today.com/popculture/jennifer-hudson-girl-behind-dream-wbna16258193.

4. *Jennifer Hudson: I'll Be Home for Christmas*, Holiday special, ABC, December 14, 2009.

Chapter One: Back to the Start

5. Quoted in Nick Curtis, "Oscar Hope Hudson Brings Down the House," *London Evening Standard*, January 25, 2007. www.standard.co.uk/go/london/film/oscar-hope-hudson-brings-down-the-house-7207014.html.

6. *Behind the Music*, "Jennifer Hudson," episode 213, VH1, June 28, 2010.

7. Quoted in Robert K. Elder, "Though Hudson's Career Took Off, Her Family Here Kept Her Grounded," *Chicago Tribune*, October 26, 2008. articles.chicagotribune.com/2008-10-26/news/0810250298_1_jennifer-hudson-hip-hop-albums-mother.

8. *Behind the Music*, "Jennifer Hudson."

9. Quoted in Curtis, "Oscar Hope Hudson Brings Down the House."

10. Quoted in Ihejirika, "Jennifer Hudson at Women's Conference: 'We Have No Choice but to Keep On Going.'"

11. Jennifer Hudson, "The Church She Calls Home," *Guideposts*, October 17, 2013. www.guideposts.org/better-living/entertainment/music/the-church-she-calls-home.

12. *Jennifer Hudson: I'll Be Home for Christmas*, Holiday special, ABC.

13. Quoted in Dave Hoekstra, "Living the Dream: Jennifer Hudson Brings Truth, Clarity to 'Dreamgirls' Role," *Chicago Sun-Times*, December 16, 2006.

14. Quoted in Hoekstra, "Living the Dream."

Chapter Two: Chasing a Dream

15. Quoted in Hoekstra, "Living the Dream."

16. Quoted in Hoekstra, "Living the Dream."

17. Quoted in *Empress*, "Jennifer Hudson—Something Like a Dream." www.danaroc.com/guests_ShaleiaJamila_022607.html.

18. Quoted in Alan Jackson, "'I'm Proof that Dreams Do Come True': Jennifer Hudson on Living the A-list Life," *MailOnline*, July 25, 2011. www.dailymail.co.uk/home/you/article-2011469/Jennifer-Hudson-living-A-list-life-Im-proof-dreams-come-true.html.

19. Quoted in *Denver Post*, "Dreamgirl's New Reality a Very Busy One Film Role, New Disc in works," May 3, 2007. www.denverpost.com/2007/05/03/dreamgirls-new-reality-a-very-busy-one-film-role-new-disc-in-works/.

Chapter Three: An American Idol

20. *American Idol*, season 3, episode 2, Fox Broadcasting Company, January 20, 2004.

21. *American Idol*, season 3, episode 9, Fox Broadcasting Company, February 10, 2004.

22. *Barbara Walters Oscar Special*, ABC, February 25, 2007.

23. *American Idol*, season 3, episode 9.

24. *American Idol*, season 3, episode 9.

25. *American Idol*, season 3, episode 18, Fox Broadcasting Company, March 9, 2004.

26. *American Idol*, season 3, episode 18.

27. Quoted in MTV News Staff, "For the Record: Quick News on Jennifer Hudson, Mixtape Awards, Andre 3000, Will Ferrell, 'Borat' & More," *MTV News*, December 8, 2006. www.mtv.com/news/1547617/for-the-record-quick-news-on-jennifer-hudson-mixtape-awards-andre-3000-will-ferrell-borat-more/.

28. Quoted in Lola Ogunnaike, "And the Mirror Says: Go for It, Dreamgirl," *New York Times*, February 25, 2007. www.nytimes.com/2007/02/25/movies/awardsseason/25hudson.html.

29. *American Idol*, season 3, episode 30, Fox Broadcasting Company, April 21, 2004.

30. *American Idol*, season 3, episode 30.

31. *American Idol*, season 3, episode 30.

32. Quoted in A. Simigis, "Reality Might: 'American Idol' Champ Fantasia Barrino Storms the Charts," *Chicago Tribune*, August 4, 2004. www.chicagotribune.com/news/ct-xpm-2004-08-04-0408050201-story.html.

33. Quoted in Associated Press, "Elton John Says 'American Idol' Vote Is 'Racist,'" *USA Today*, April 28, 2004. www.usatoday.com/life/people/2004-04-28-elton-john-idol_x.htm.

34. *Behind the Music*, "Jennifer Hudson."

35. Quoted in Scholastic, "Profiles of American Idol Top Ten." www.scholastic.com/browse/article.jsp?id=5383.

Chapter Four: Dream, Work, Do

36. Roger Ebert, "Ebert's Oscar Predictions," RogerEbert.com, February 10, 2007. www.rogerebert.com/festivals-and-awards/eberts-oscar-predictions-2007.

37. Peter Travers, "Dreamgirls," *Rolling Stone*, November 21, 2006. www.rollingstone.com/movies/reviews/dreamgirls-20061121.

38. Hudson, interview by David Letterman, *The Late Show with David Letterman*.

39. Jennifer Hudson acceptance speech, *79th Academy Awards*, ABC, February 25, 2007.

40. Manohla Dargis, "The Girls Are Back in Town," *New York Times*, May 30, 2008. www.nytimes.com/2008/05/30/movies/30sex. html.

41. Ramin Setoodeh, "Criticism of 'Sex and the City' Is Mostly Sexist," *Newsweek*, June 2, 2008. www.newsweek.com/criticism-sex-and-city-mostly-sexist-91019.

42. Carina Chocano, "Review: 'Sex and the City," *Los Angeles Times*, May 30, 2008. www.latimes.com/entertainment/la-et-sex30-2008may30-story.html.

43. A. O. Scott, "A Golden Dollop of Motherly Comfort," *New York Times*, October 17, 2008. movies.nytimes.com/2008/10/17/movies/17bees.html.

44. Roger Ebert, "The Secret Life of Bees," RogerEbert.com, October 15, 2008. www.rogerebert.com/reviews/the-secret-life-of-bees-2008.

45. Rotten Tomatoes, "The Secret Life of Bees (2008)." www.rottentomatoes.com/m/secret_life_of_bees.

46. *Barbara Walters Oscar Special*, ABC, February 25, 2007.

47. *Barbara Walters Oscar Special*, ABC, February 25, 2007.

Chapter Five: Hard to Say Goodbye

48. *The Early Show*, CBS News, October 27, 2008.

49. *The Early Show*, CBS News, October 27, 2008.

50. Quoted in Alex Starritt, "Jennifer Hudson 'Remained Strong' as She Identified Shot Nephew," *Telegraph*, October 28, 2008. www.telegraph.co.uk/news/worldnews/northamerica/usa/.3273698/Jennifer-Hudson-remained-strong-as-she-identified-shot-nephew.html.

51. Quoted in Daniel Kreps, "Jennifer Hudson's Family Killed In 'Jealous Rage,' Say Prosecutors," *Rolling Stone*, December 4, 2008. www.rollingstone.com/music/music-news/jennifer-hudsons-family-killed-in-jealous-rage-say-prosecutors-93421/.

52. Quoted in Kreps, "Jennifer Hudson's Family Killed In 'Jealous Rage,' Say Prosecutors."

53. Quoted in Daniel Kreps, "Cowell, Abdul Send Condolences to Jennifer Hudson," *Rolling Stone*, October 28, 2008. www.rollingstone.com/music/music-news/cowell-abdul-send-condolences-to-jennifer-hudson-95194/.

54. Quoted in Associated Press, "Private Funeral Held for Hudson Family," NBCNews.com, November 3, 2008.

55. Quoted in Josh Grossberg, "Jennifer Hudson on Her Family' s Tragic Murder: 'I Was Outside of Myself,'" *E! News*, June 29, 2010. www.eonline.com/news/188125/jennifer-hudson-on-her-family-s-tragic-murder-i-was-outside-of-myself.

56. Quoted in Grossberg, "Jennifer Hudson on her Family's Tragic Murder."

Chapter Six: Moving Forward

57. Quoted in William Goodman, "Jennifer Hudson Lip-Synched Super Bowl Performance," *SPIN*, February 2, 2009. www.spin.com/2009/02/jennifer-hudson-lip-synched-super-bowl-performance/.

58. *Behind the Music*, "Jennifer Hudson."

59. *Behind the Music*, "Jennifer Hudson."

60. Quoted in Shirley Halperin, "Dave Grohl, Coldplay, Jennifer Hudson Lead All-Star Tribute to Neil Diamond at MusiCares Gala," *Rolling Stone*, February 7, 2009. www.rollingstone.com/music/music-news/dave-grohl-coldplay-jennifer-hudson-lead-all-star-tribute-to-neil-diamond-at-musicares-gala-86655/.

61. Quoted in Ree Hines, "Jennifer Hudson Tells Oprah She's Forgiven Family's Killer: 'It's Not His Fault,'" Today.com, September 10, 2012. www.today.com/popculture/jennifer-hudson-tells-oprah-shes-forgiven-familys-killer-its-not-989957.

62. Quoted in Leanne Bayley, "Jennifer Hudson Credits Her Son for Saving Her Life," *Glamour*, October 8, 2015. www.glamourmagazine.co.uk/article/jennifer-hudson-interview-glamour-magazine-2015.

63. *Behind the Music*, "Jennifer Hudson."

64. Quoted in Gil Kaufman, "Jennifer Hudson Signs with Epic Records," *Billboard*, June 28, 2016. www.billboard.com/articles/columns/pop/7423121/jennifer-hudson-signs-with-epic-records-deal.

65. Quoted in Elyse Dupre, "Jennifer Hudson Says It's Always Been Her Dream to Play Aretha Franklin," *E! News*, September 26, 2018. www.eonline.com/news/971591/jennifer-hudson-says-it-s-always-been-her-dream-to-play-aretha-franklin.

66. Quoted in Ihejirika, "Jennifer Hudson at Women's Conference: 'We Have No Choice but to Keep On Going.'"

Jennifer Hudson Year by Year

1981

Jennifer Kate Hudson is born September 12 in Chicago, Illinois.

1998

Hudson's beloved grandmother, Julia Kate Hudson, dies.

1999

Hudson graduates from high school; she begins dating James Payton, a relationship that will last for eight years; she briefly attends Langston University before transferring to Kennedy-King College; and her stepfather, Samuel Simpson, dies.

2001

Hudson is cast in Chicago's Marriott Lincolnshire Theatre's production of the musical *Big River*, in which she performs for nearly two years; she drops out of college to devote herself to her singing career; and her sister gives birth to Jennifer's nephew, Julian King.

2003

Hudson performs the role of Calliope in *Hercules: The Musical*, a Disney cruise ship production; she turns down a second contract with Disney to audition for *American Idol*.

2004

Hudson appears on season 3 of *American Idol*, makes it to the finals, and is eliminated in seventh place; she subsequently tours the United States with the American Idol Live! tour and appears on Broadway in the one-night Actors Fund of America benefit performance of the rock musical *Hair*.

2006

Hudson appears in *Dreamgirls*.

2007

Hudson wins the Academy Award for Best Supporting Actress and becomes the first African American singer and only the third African American celebrity to appear on the cover of *Vogue* magazine.

2008

Hudson appears in the movies *Sex and the City* and *The Secret Life of Bees*, releases the album *Jennifer Hudson*, and becomes engaged to David Otunga; her mother, brother, and nephew are murdered in Chicago.

2009

Hudson performs at Super Bowl XLIII; appears in *Fragments*; wins a Grammy Award for best rhythm and blues album; and gives birth to her son, David Daniel Otunga Jr.

2011

Hudson plays controversial South African politician Winnie Mandela in biopic *Winnie* and releases her second album, *I Remember Me*.

2013

Hudson appears on the television show *Smash* and in *Black Nativity*.

2014

Hudson releases album *JHUD* and guest stars on the hit show *Empire*.

2015

Hudson stars as Shug in the Broadway version of *The Color Purple* and wins another Grammy for her contribution to the show's soundtrack.

2016

Hudson stars as Motormouth Maybelle in *Hairspray! Live* on NBC and joins the judges panel for *The Voice UK*.

2017

Hudson separates from partner David Otunga and releases the lead single from her next album, called "Remember Me."

2018

Hudson performs at the March for Our Lives and announces that she will play Grizabella in the film version of the musical *Cats* as well as playing Aretha Franklin in a film that was given the tentative title *Respect*.

For More Information

Books

Bejaminson, Peter. *The Lost Supreme: The Life of Dreamgirl Florence Ballard*. Chicago, IL: Lawrence Hill Books, 2008.
This book delves into the life of Florence Ballard, the inspiration for Hudson's Oscar-winning role of Effie White.

Kidd, Sue Monk. *The Secret Life of Bees*. New York, NY: Penguin, 2002.
This novel about family secrets and life in the South in the early 1960s was adapted into a movie starring Queen Latifah, Alicia Keys, Dakota Fanning, and Jennifer Hudson.

Nagle, Jeanne. *Jennifer Hudson*. New York, NY: Rosen Publishing, 2008.
This biography of Jennifer Hudson describes her rise to national prominence as a singer on reality television.

West, Betsy. *Jennifer Hudson: American Dream Girl*. New York, NY: Price Stern Sloan, 2007.
This book explores Hudson's stint on *American Idol* and her success in her debut film, *Dreamgirls*.

Websites

Jennifer Hudson on Twitter
(twitter.com/IAMJHUD)
Jennifer Hudson's official Twitter account shares news about the singer's music, her appearances on *The Voice*, and of course, thoughts about her daily life.

Jennifer Hudson on YouTube
(www.youtube.com/channel/UCrdLOfTvb9EKlyRoJTMVNgQ)
Jennifer's official YouTube channel houses her music videos, live performances, and behind-the-scenes videos of making her albums.

Julian D. King Gift Foundation
(www.juliandkinggiftfoundation.com)
The Julian D. King Gift Foundation website has information about Julian's life, foundation news, and ways to get involved in Chicago events.

Index

Picture Credits

About the Author

Edna McPhee wanted to be an astronaut when she grew up, but when NASA stopped sending people to the moon she decided to become a writer instead. She has written for a variety of different publications as journalist and short-story writer. She currently lives in the mountains of Colorado with her two dogs, named Tom and Jerry, and an entire room filled with knitting yarn. She still wants to go to the moon.